From the Farm to the Boardroom:

Leadership Lessons

By Rita Lowman

Published by Richter Publishing LLC www.richterpublishing.com

Editors: Mandi Weems, Nicole Dentremont & Elizabeth Foulke

Additional Contributors: Akil Small & Diana Fisler

ISBN:1945812036
ISBN-13:9781945812033

DISCLAIMER

This book is designed to provide information on leadership and business only. This information is provided and sold with the knowledge that the publisher and author do not offer any legal or medical advice. In the case of a need for any such expertise, consult with the appropriate professional. This book does not contain all information available on the subject. This book has not been created to be specific to any individual's or organization's situation or needs. Every effort has been made to make this book as accurate as possible. However, there may be typographical and/ or content errors. Therefore, this book should serve only as a general guide and not as the ultimate source of subject information. This book contains information that might be dated and is intended only to educate and entertain. The author and publisher shall have no liability or responsibility to any person or entity regarding any loss or damage incurred, or alleged to have incurred, directly or indirectly, by the information contained in this book. You hereby agree to be bound by this disclaimer or you may return this book within the guarantee time period for a full refund. This book contains names of companies and their practices. While the author and publisher take no responsibility for the business practices of these companies and or the performance of any product or service, the author or publisher has used the product or service and makes a recommendation in good faith based on that experience. All characters appearing in this work are fictitious unless properly cited. Any resemblance to other similar persons, living or dead, is purely coincidental. All opinions in the book are only of the author only and not that of the publishing house.

DEDICATION

This book is dedicated to my family: Gary, Gary Jr, Clint, and Brock. Thank you for always being there for me and encouraging me along the way.

Being a family means you are a part of something very wonderful. It means you will love and be loved for the rest of your Life no matter what.

"Family: where life begins and love never ends."

ACKNOWLEDGMENTS

There are so many people that have helped and inspired me along the way. One of my mentors, Alex Sink, always gave the encouragement to do whatever I set my mind to do.

THE HEART OF MENTORING: GETTING THE MOST OUT OF LIFE ISN'T ABOUT HOW MUCH YOU KEEP FOR YOURSELF BUT HOW MUCH YOU POUR INTO OTHERS.

My husband, who has stood by me for over 45 years, was one of the driving forces behind me writing this book. After talking about some of the things I have accomplished in life, he said "Put it all on paper and make it a reality, because not only will it be self-satisfying for you, but it will give others some ideas of things to do as they continue to grow in their careers and in their life." Thank you for always inspiring me.

THE RELATIONSHIP BETWEEN HUSBAND AND WIFE SHOULD BE ONE OF CLOSEST FRIENDS. GARY HAS AND ALWAYS WILL BE MY CLOSEST AND BEST FRIEND.

CONTENTS

"PEOPLE KNOW YOUR NAME, NOT YOUR STORY. THEY'VE HEARD YOUR SUCCESS AND WHAT YOU HAVE ACCOMPLISHED, BUT NOT WHAT YOU'VE BEEN THROUGH. SO TAKE THEIR OPINIONS AS JUST THAT, OPINIONS. IN THE END, IT IS NOT ABOUT WHAT OTHERS THINK, IT IS WHAT YOU THINK OF YOURSELF THAT COUNTS. YOU HAVE TO DO WHAT IS BEST FOR YOUR LIFE, AND NOT WHAT IS BEST FOR EVERYONE ELSE."

INTRODUCTION

"From the Farm to the Boardroom: Leadership Lessons" is an inspirational book taking you on a journey with a girl from a quaint small town to big city banking. I share with you my lessons learned along the way on how to flourish from any situation. In order to become successful, you cannot let anything hold you back. It's not where you come from, but where you are going that makes all the difference.

CHAPTER 1: GROWING UP

When I was nine years old I stood before a judge, tasked with making one of the most difficult decisions a young child can make: did I want to live with my mother or my father? Terrified of upsetting my parents, I struggled to make the right choice. If I chose my mother, would my father no longer love me? If I chose my father, would my mother feel betrayed? I looked up at the judge in his black robe and told him that I wanted to live with both. I would live with my mother during the week and my father from Fridays through Sundays.

I was born in Columbus, Georgia, a lovely town on the Chattahoochee River. When I was growing up, Columbus was a relatively small town. Old wooden houses with wraparound porches and live oak lined the streets

My parents attended high school together and were married when my dad returned from serving in the army. He worked as a fireman and my mom was a housewife. I was their only child. However, when I was two years old, they realized that they couldn't live together happily, so they divorced.

This was in the late 1950s so it was more of a rarity to come from a broken home. There weren't many other kids at school whose parents had divorced so sometimes I wondered if there was something about me that was lacking. Like all children of divorce, I thought that if I had just done something differently than my parents would still be together. At other times, I would look at the home lives of my classmates and friends and wish to have both of my parents living together under the same roof. It would have been easy for me to feel sorry for myself or to use my home situation as a crutch and an excuse to withdraw from life. But I was fortunate. My family provided love and care and others were placed in my life who served as mentors. They were beacons of light providing guidance and they've been my roots, offering lifelong support.

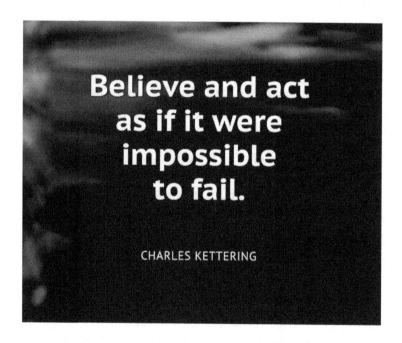

Believe and act as if it were impossible to fail.

CHARLES KETTERING

After my parents divorced, my mother and I spent several years living with my grandmother. I don't remember too much from my early years, but when I think of my grandmother I am flooded with warm thoughts.

Perhaps we are drawn to people when we are young because we sense that they see something in us that we do not yet know exists within ourselves. For me, my fourth grade teacher, Leah Caldwell became an early role model. I got off to somewhat of a rocky start in elementary school. I remember being teased for being tall and wearing glasses. As kids we know little of self-esteem. Our peers' words, when they are cruel, can ruin our whole day or even a whole year. I'm not sure what life would have been like had I not had the good fortune to be placed in Mrs. Caldwell's class. Though I couldn't yet see it myself, Mrs. Caldwell saw in me the makings of a leader. In class she pushed me to speak and share my ideas. I learned to become comfortable expressing my thoughts to others rather than keeping quiet. At the time it wasn't like I thought of this as a leadership trait. I just knew it felt good to speak up and have my voice heard.

IT ISN'T WHERE YOU CAME FROM, IT'S WHERE YOU'RE GOING THAT COUNTS.

— ELLA FITZGERALD

Photo: Shutterstock

Leah introduced me to 4-H. This is where I got my first taste of hard physical work and also where I learned the importance of giving back to one's community. Some of my earliest and fondest memories are of the summer after my fourth-grade year. Leah encouraged me to go to camp and I spent my first nights away from home. I attended the Rock Eagle 4-H camp. We slept in wooden cabins and smelled the pine and earth. I loved being out in nature. Here I also had my first opportunity to serve in a leadership role. I was elected President of my 4-H club. I loved the feeling of being trusted with extra responsibility. It meant that people saw something in me that led them to believe they could count on me. I wanted to prove to them that they were right and I was able to rise to the occasion.

People who shine from within, don't need the spotlight.

Positive Outlooks

Several years after my parents' divorce, when I was about six, both of my parents remarried. So in that courtroom, forced to state who I wanted to live with, it was not merely my mother and father I was deciding between because by this time I also had stepparents. The fact that I chose to spend time with both my mother and father is a testimony to what wonderful people my stepparents were. Mine wasn't the life of Cinderella, forced to slave away for a never-satisfied stepmother. I was loved, yet I was also taught a strong work ethic.

You have to do what is right for *yourself* nobody else is *walking* in your shoes

My father and stepmother always had me do chores. I would do the dishes or help my stepmother by dusting and folding the laundry. When I was young I even worked with my father, helping him with construction on the weekends. Today I suppose there are some who may see this as a harsh upbringing. Yet I am grateful for these weekends working with my father. It's here where I could really begin to understand that tasks do not get accomplished by themselves. We often see the end result without stopping to reflect on all of the small and sometimes tedious tasks that go into creating a final project. To build a house, there is a lot of precise measuring that requires attention to detail. There's also the physical labor of pounding nails and holding up 2 by 4s. As I began to get an understanding of the work, I also learned how satisfying it is to give something your all and to see the results.

Never hope for it more than you work for it.

AUTHOR
SONYA TECLAI
THEGOODVIBE.CO

I lived a modest life but my family sacrificed their time in order to support my dreams. One of my early passions in life was dance. I found it to be a way to express some of the bottled up emotions that I was feeling through motion and creativity. My stepmother saw how important this outlet was for me. As a stepdaughter, I wasn't the one forced to sew and mend; my stepmother, who was a wonderful seamstress, made me clothes and dance outfits. Through this act of kindness, I knew I was supported and loved.

The two households that I grew up in were very different. In my mother's home, I did not do chores. She wanted to do everything for me. It felt weird to sit at the table and have my dishes cleared and plates washed for me. They too knew how important dancing was for me. While my stepmother made my dresses, my mother and stepfather would sometimes buy me very expensive dresses for events and would pay for me to be in pageants. As a child, I understood that this put a financial strain on my parents' finances. Today I appreciate and understand the sacrifices. As an adult, I realize that my mother strove to give me more than she could afford. Now a parent myself, I know there are certain things we want for our children despite the cost. I see the sacrifices my parents made so that I would not have to go without.

In junior high, I once again found myself standing before a black-cloaked judge. My stepfather was stationed in Hawaii and he and my mom were moving there. But I knew that I needed to stay in Georgia. I was already beginning to sense the opportunity that awaited me if I stayed. Though it pained me to ask the judge to allow me to stay with my father, as I knew this was a hard blow for my mother, I listened to the inner voice which was telling me to stay. The year without my mom was one that allowed me to grow and build inner-strength.

My mom and stepfather moved back and my parents homes we're about five blocks apart from each other. I was thrilled because now I could continue to jump on my bike and ride the short blocks between them. During holidays I could spend Christmas Eve at one of my parents' houses and then in the morning, pedal over to find the tree with its shining lights in my other home with my family waiting.

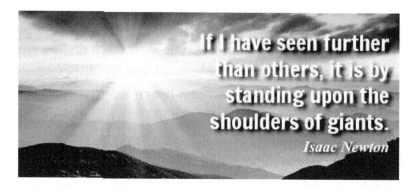

If I have seen further than others, it is by standing upon the shoulders of giants.
Isaac Newton

In junior high, I decided to run for president of student council. Ever since my time as President of 4-H at Rock Eagle , I was drawn to leadership positions. I was captain of the cheerleading squad and loved stepping up to the responsibility that this entailed. The fact that I was a girl who was running for the position of student council president, was secondary to my desire to see what changes I could make to better the school. I probably felt we needed better water fountains and more dances. Nothing can describe the thrill I felt when I won. It showed that my classmates believed in my abilities. I was eager to make good on my campaign promises. And when I won, there was the extra sense of accomplishment and honor of being the first girl in our school to be elected as student council president.

Transitioning to high school from junior high was interesting because there were three high schools in our area and the junior high kids were split between the three. I had made a group of friends who I bonded with strongly in junior high. I dreaded going to high school and leaving my friends behind. Would I have anyone to sit with at lunch? And if not, how would I make it through school, alone? I imagined many scenarios.

I suppose, like many, my eyes were opened to the ways of the world in high school. Perhaps I had been naïve in junior high. My successes in school government and cheer and the great friendships I made showed me a side of life where people were kind and open. Furthermore, the fact that my parents had been able to remain friendly and provide me with a stable childhood despite their divorce, taught me that people can push aside their differences in order to work together for a common goal. So it was somewhat of a shock when I found that in high school, people split up into groups and separated themselves by these groups. It seemed that sometime people chose to be in one group over another and at other times, perhaps unfairly, the choice was one that was made for them. This exposed me to the political nature of life—and I don't mean the kind of politics we see in our legislative or presidential campaign. I had always seen school as a place where people went to receive an education, to join clubs and activities. But I began to realize that others saw school in different terms. There was a social element that seemed to override all else.

I was sometimes left out of activities because of my strict home life. I had an 11 o'clock curfew which prevented me from participating in a lot of the activities that other kids were part of on weekends. I wanted to go out to the movies or to a dance. I could as long as I returned home by 11 o'clock. On Monday mornings it seemed like my friends would be talking about the great time they had. But I had a strong desire to make my parents happy and so I adhered to my curfew because I didn't want to disappoint my dad.

Choosing to follow my family's rules rather than being part of the social scene had consequences. I didn't feel as connected to my peers as I had in junior high. This could have made me cynical. Sadly, so many of us do become a little jaded when we are teens; this might occur for different reasons. Yet somehow, in high school I learned the importance of forgiveness. Again, an intuitive though, showed me a truth: We don't forgive others because they deserve it; we forgive for our own peace of mind and spirit.

Sometimes you have to do what's best for you and your life, not what's best for everybody else.

HpLyrikz.com

I don't want it to come across as if high school was a dark time in my life. I continued to search for opportunities to serve in leadership positions. I had the pleasure of being a class officer in the homecoming court and lieutenant colonel of ROTC.

One of the biggest lessons that I learned in high school was the importance of finding a mentor—someone to look up to for guidance. Fortunately for me, several people were placed in my life in my younger years who served as inspiration.

In junior high school, Neva Gran, the mother of one of my classmates stepped in and served as something of a surrogate mom. This was when my mom was in Hawaii. Neva had four of her own children, yet she was always able to make me feel like part of the family. Though I had my father and stepmom, I found that I missed my own mother terribly and Neva served as another maternal figure during those years when young girls are vulnerable and in need of strong female role models. She played an active role in my activities, even assisting me when I ran for Babe Ruth Queen. Neva treated me as one of her own children and this was integral in building my self-esteem. Though I had days I struggled, it was the acceptance I received from Neva that helped me to push through on some of the tough days.

In high school, I met the man who was to become my husband, though of course I hadn't a clue that we would spend our lives together when we first met. He was from the city of Atlanta, a place I had never been. My family vacations consisted of going to Panama City or St. Augustine, Florida. That was the furthest from home I'd ever gone. We met in September and began dating in December of '69. More about Gary later.

It is those relationships that I have made along the way that have really set me to be who I am today. Looking back on these memories, I can see that those things made a difference in my life.

"THE BEST THINGS IN LIFE ARE THE PEOPLE YOU LOVE, THE PLACES YOU HAVE SEEN, AND THE MEMORIES YOU'VE MADE ALONG THE WAY."

CHAPTER 2: BANKING BECOMES A CAREER

When I was a little girl, I loved to dance. It wasn't merely the freedom I felt, leaping through the air and twirling across the wooden boards of the studio; dance, was an outlet for the bottled up emotions I held inside. Just beneath the surface, they threatened to explode into anger at times. The physical exertion dance demanded, the attention to the precise moves of the routine my teacher had just called out, these served as a sort of meditation that allowed for a respite from my troubled teenage storm. But there was something else I loved about dance—the performance. Beyond the inner relief it gave, I loved to participate in pageants and dance recitals. It thrilled me to feel the theatre full of eyes on me; I could almost hear the intake of breath as we dancers executed a tentative pirouette.

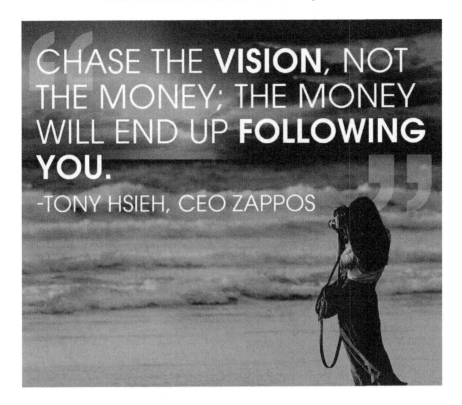

Later, I started acting and performed in a few plays at our local theatre. I dreamt of moving to Hollywood or Broadway and making it big. Here, my audience wouldn't merely be the people I bumped into at the grocery store in Columbus, they'd be people from across the country, crowding in lines to see my latest film. But my dreams were tempered by a more practical side. I knew I would have to earn a living. I looked around at my options, and found an interest in banking.

IN THE END,
WE ONLY
REGRET
THE CHANCES
WE DIDN'T
TAKE.

As it happened, I was able to use some of the skills that I acquired as student council president and lieutenant colonel of ROTC in my new position. I was placed in charge of opening new banking centers and attending the grand openings. I loved the festive atmosphere and the excitement this generated in the customers and employees. Banks exude an aura of formality. The brass bars, ionic columns ad marble counters demand a certain element of reverence and respect. But banks are also places of possibility, where teens with their first babysitting or lifeguard jobs come to open their first checking accounts, where newlyweds come when purchasing their first home. This wasn't acting, yet it still coursed with life.

My duties included training new employees and being a type of ambassador for the bank. Here, my early years of training at Rock Eagle came in handy. I found I had a talent for communicating with people. Many people feel uncomfortable sharing with others what to do; they might feel that people should just know what to do without having to be told. But I have always looked at management in a similar light to coaching. Mrs. Caldwell had modeled this for me at an early age, when she pushed me to speak up in class. I believe that people are not always able to tap into their unique talents without guidance and instruction from others. So for me, when I train others, I see it as helping them to grow, not only in their jobs, but in their confidence. Also banking was a way to allow me to attend college and other banking schools. The positive was the education was funded by the bank.

My work in the bank did not go unnoticed. A newspaper found my story interesting and wrote an article on me. They were impressed by the fact that I was able to rise so quickly in this profession at such a young age. It was also rather rare for a woman to be holding such a visible position at a bank. I remember one of the interview questions they asked: "What do you want to do in your career?" At the time, I answered that I wanted to be senior vice president of the bank. I was in my 20s and this seemed as big of a dream that I could achieve. I think it odd now that the most I thought to reach for was senior vice president. Why not president? Similarly to the way in which I hadn't considered college early in my life, I was incapable of imagining the places a career in banking could take me. The newspaper considered me a trailblazer and how accurate this was I couldn't begin to know. For this implied that I was off on a course in which there were no footsteps to follow. Part of the reason I couldn't conceive of being a president of the bank was because there simply were no female bank presidents. It's hard to stretch one's imagination to those things which have yet to exist. So it was a series of small steps that brought me to the boardroom.

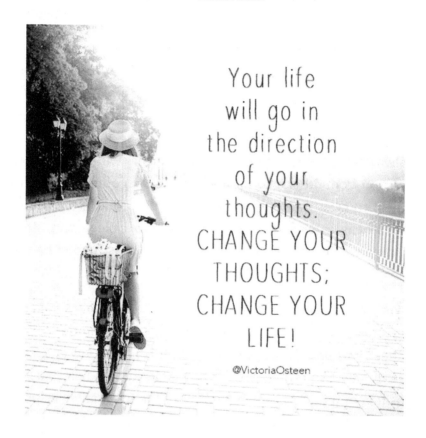

Your life
will go in
the direction
of your
thoughts.
CHANGE YOUR
THOUGHTS;
CHANGE YOUR
LIFE!

@VictoriaOsteen

Meanwhile, my husband's own career at Kraft Foods was taking off. We began to think about starting a family. After trying to conceive with no success, we decided to see a doctor. I hoped that there wouldn't be any news. "Nothing wrong," the doctor would say, "just keep trying you two," but this was not the case. I learned that we might never be able to conceive children. In the doctor's office time seemed to fold in on itself. As a woman, it felt as though I had just learned there was something defective in me. What did it matter if my career was taking off, I would never be able to do the one thing that a woman is supposed to do. I would never give birth. Rationally, I could tell myself that my life still had purpose, that I was a career woman married to a wonderful man. But this went beyond reason and cut into my very sense of self.

Gary knew I was devastated. He looked for a way to show me that his love for me was not dependent on our ability to have children. As a sign of his support and his wish to ease my pain, he bought me a ring. All these years later, I look down at my hand to see the ring as I type this.

We decided to look into adoption because we knew we wanted a family. As an only child, I had always dreamed of having a house full of my own children. I remembered the energy and noise of the Gran household with its four kids bumping into furniture, shouting down the hallways and crowding the dinner table. To me, this was the vision of what I wanted our home to be.

As the adoption process chugged along, I woke one morning feeling sick. I didn't think much of it and continued getting ready for my job at the bank. This continued but it never occurred to me that I might be pregnant. The doctor had seemed pretty adamant that we would not be able to conceive. Gary and I had been praying for a child, yet we trusted that our child might come to us through adoption. We could scarcely believe it when we learned I was pregnant.

Sometimes life's timing seems too perfectly orchestrated to be mere coincidence. The day after I learned I was pregnant we received a call from our attorney letting us know they had a child for us. We were torn. Should we have faith that the pregnancy was what God wanted for us, or should we not take the risk and proceed with the adoption process? Once again, I found myself facing a seemingly impossible decision. Yet this time I had a partner with me and though I was anxious and afraid to make the wrong decision, I saw that being able to walk through such a dilemma with the man I loved eased my soul. Gary and I believed that this pregnancy was a gift and that by not adopting, we might give another family, also hoping for a child, the opportunity to start their own family. We made our decision and two days before Christmas I gave birth to a healthy baby boy. When the doctor placed him in my arms and I felt his tiny body fill with breath next to mine, I could hardly believe it possible that we had a family of three.

I was only able to stay home for 11 days before I had to go back to work. I struggled with this decision because I had waited so long for child and now I would have to leave him to go into the office. Compounded with my own sadness and doubt in leaving Gary Jr., there was more of a stigma at this time for women who chose to continue their careers rather than stay at home to raise children. Fortunately, my mother lived near us and so she was able to care for our son until he was old enough to go to our church nursery school.

After my son's birth, Gary and I were told that the chances of having a second child were slim to none. We were so grateful to have had a child when we had thought this an impossibility, that we accepted Gary Jr. would be our only child. Once more, we were surprised and 21 months later I gave birth to a second son.

SOMETIMES LIFE IS ABOUT RISKING EVERYTHING FOR A DREAM THAT NO ONE CAN SEE BUT YOU.

We began to settle into the routine of being two working parents with two young sons. As I said, my mother was close and she was able to help out. But In 1983 Gary received an opportunity for a promotion. This meant we would leave Georgia, the state where we had both spent all of our lives, and move to Florida. In this case, there really wasn't much of a question of what the right thing to do was. Gary took the promotion and the four of us headed south.

Christmas of 1983 we headed back up to Georgia so that we could spend the holidays with our family. We were glad to be close enough to all be together. On the return drive to Florida, we had just pulled onto the highway when all of sudden, at the crest of a hill, the glare of another car's headlights shone directly into our front windshield. I remember the screech of tires on the pavement and the shattering of glass. People say that your life flashes before your eyes in a near-death experience but all I could think about was Gary and my children. I lost consciousness in the crash so much of what I know of it is from what others told me afterwards.

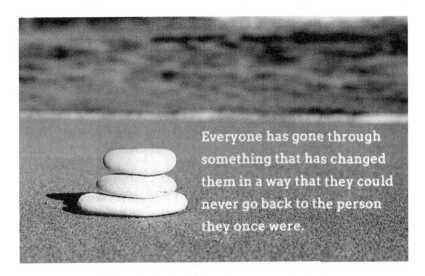

Everyone has gone through something that has changed them in a way that they could never go back to the person they once were.

Gary had been able to pull our boys out of the car to safety. The crash left him with fractured ribs and a ruptured spleen. I was trapped in the car, the motor pushed into my right side. Gary had no choice but to wait for the EMTs to arrive and hope that they would be able to pry me out with the Jaws of Life.

My parents had received a phone call telling them of the crash. Off they rushed to the hospital but when they tried to see me, they discovered that I was not yet at the hospital. In a panic, my mother drove near the site of the accident, only to be told there had been a serious accident and traffic was being stopped. Not realizing who my mother was, the EMTs told her, "there's a woman trapped in the car and we don't know if we can get her out." As a mother myself, my first thought when I regained consciousness was of my boys. I knew that if I was hurt this badly, the chances that Gary and the boys were also severely injured was fairly likely.

I tried to remain hopeful, yet my mind raced to a dark place. Could it be that after finally being filled with the love of my own children, after a couple of short years of life they were to be taken from me? I could hardly bear to think these thoughts and they were more insidious than the pain from the crash.

At the hospital, I searched the faces of the nurses and surgeons for a clue about my family's well-being. Yet I was unable to discern anything from the faces behind the surgical masks. As the doctor began to prep me for surgery, he talked to me of the importance of having a clear mind before going under. There was no way for my mind to be at rest until I knew of the fate of my husband and children. The relief I felt when they allowed Gary and the boys to step in to the prep room – I saw my boys' smiling faces and this eased my troubled mind and I was wheeled down the corridor to surgery.

Gary's injuries put him in the hospital for the next three days, but mine were so severe that I had to remain for five weeks. I had several broken bones and my right leg had to be completely rebuilt. When we were finally able to return to Florida, I had to learn to walk again.

I was told that I would only have usage of 70% of my right side. This at first was devastating for me, who had once found such solace in dance and cheer. There is so much that we take for granted on a daily basis, being able to walk down the grocery aisle, to bend over and pick up our children's toys. When we can no longer do them, these things we often complain about become the tasks we long to engage in once more. I was determined to walk again and in 11 months I went from wheelchair to walker to crutches. I learned how to compensate for that part of my body which I never regained full use of. To this day, people don't realize that I do not have full usage of my body.

Retraining myself to walk, working with a physical therapist was often a laborious task. To struggle to do something that was once so simple was humbling and I had to remind myself not to become too frustrated when the progress was slower than I wanted. In order to distract myself from my physical condition, I returned to my job at the advertising agency where I'd been working since our move to Florida.

My job in the advertising agency soon led to work for a congressional campaign. I handled the PR, speaking engagements and appearances for the candidate in his district. This work reminded me of what I loved so much about the bank openings. There is something about the energy of a crowd that is intoxicating. The world of finance and the world of politics are both filled with possibility. Like the helium-filled balloons at the rallies, hope pushes out from within beckoning us to follow it upwards, when we encounter a candidate who speaks to our own beliefs and dreams.

While working on the campaign, I was introduced to an executive of the North Carolina National Bank (NCNB). The company had recently moved into Florida. My talent and skillset impressed the executive and I was soon offered a position. Though I had loved the brief time I spent in the realm of politics, the world of banking called to me. I couldn't wait to be back in a marketing role similar to the one I'd had in Georgia. But I didn't stay in marketing for long. I soon moved up and became the Advertising Director of NCNB for Florida.

One of the tasks in my new position was to bring a local feel to the bank since it came from the Carolinas into Florida. We immediately began a campaign that featured local people and local clients. I think it can be easy to forget sometimes that banking is ultimately about people. What is presented to the public is, at its core, a means to connect and feel part of a community. It is essential that we trust the institution where we choose to place our hard-earned money. On a more personal level, I've come to understand that the way in which I present myself is integral to my own professional and personal growth.

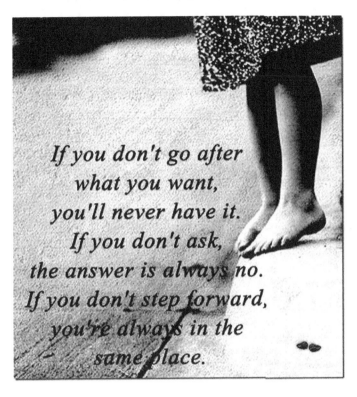

If you don't go after what you want, you'll never have it. If you don't ask, the answer is always no. If you don't step forward, you're always in the same place.

During my early marketing days, one of the things that I learned and carry with me to this day is: "Your smile is your logo, your personality is your business card, and how you leave others after an experience with you becomes your trademark." In one sense this means that when we work for a company we become associated with the brand of that company. But in another sense it is really ourselves that's the brand. Our success in opening up new branches, was not just because the bank I worked for was a successful brand, it was because the people who I interacted with were able to gain a sense of trust and care as a result of working with me. What's interesting is that when we focus on how we can connect with our clients, this behavior does not go unnoticed by our managers. By following my creed and striving to make others feel valued as a result of their interactions with me, I received a call from one of the executive vice presidents informing me that he would like me to become a banking manager.

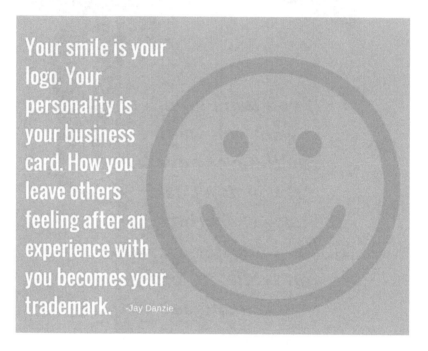

Your smile is your logo. Your personality is your business card. How you leave others feeling after an experience with you becomes your trademark. -Jay Danzie

At first I was hesitant to accept this new positions. I felt unqualified because I didn't have any experience with lending, managing people, or calling on clients. But the executive vice president assured me that the technical skills could be taught, it was the people skills that they were hiring me for.

I have always been intrigued by challenges, from my junior high days when I ran for class office, to my first job in banking. Accepting the job led to more growth and opportunity. My next stop with NCNB was as the manager of the second largest banking center in the state of Florida. I had worked in this center previously as a support person, but never as a manager. I was now responsible for the tellers, service reps, safe deposit, attendants and assistant manager. On the one hand I was nervous to return to a place where I had previously worked in this new supervisory position. How might my former colleagues respond to this? I feared it might be hard for me to take on an authoritative role if necessary. Yet the other side of me was excited for my new position, and I had confidence in my ability to perform my role well. After all, the executive vice president believed in my ability. Though now an adult, I found myself in need of the same type of champions who had rooted me on in childhood. I think anytime we embark on something new, it is infinitely easier when there are people who see what we are capable of and who encourage us to see this same potential in ourselves. So when on my second day I was presented with a challenge, I had no doubt that I would be able to walk my way through it because of the confidence others have expressed in me throughout my career.

I arrived at my office and was greeted by a group of men in business suits. These were auditors and the first thing they did was ask for my keys and my combos. I was flustered by their request yet somehow I thought to say, "When I first come in every morning I always say hello to my team, and I will get back to you in just a few moments with your request."

I asked them to wait in the conference room and in the meantime I turned to a colleague to ask her what the auditors were asking for. She steered me in the direction of the assistant manager who, she assured me, had the perfect skillset to work with the auditors. I can't quantify how beneficial it has been for me to listen to others and to be open to taking their suggestions and advice. We might have the urge to take charge anytime we can because, I think, there is an inherent fear that those of us in leadership positions have that if we don't do it ourselves, it won't get done correctly. That's what draws us to these positions in the first place, the belief that we have the ability to execute tasks successfully. And we do. But as we move up the ladder, there is no way we can take on all of the tasks that need to be completed. And here is where this other side of leadership must kick in, the ability to delegate and share the workload. Once again, I found the vastly positive effects that come from tasking others with responsibility. The assistant manager worked with the auditors professionally and with integrity. Watching her rise to the occasion, seeing the confidence it instilled in her to be handed responsibility and to meet this challenge successfully, added a deeper level of fulfillment to my own job. It is humbling to admit that there are others who are superstars in their position. It reminds me that we are all just one part of a larger whole.

"CALL ME CRAZY, BUT I LOVE TO SEE OTHER PEOPLE HAPPY AND SUCCEEDING."

The experience with the auditors actually served as a the beginning of a wonderful partnership with my assistant manager. Our bank was in Winter Haven, Florida which is filled with lakes. Early on I realized that I wanted to blend bank with community and we brainstormed ways that we might do this. Boating is very popular in Winter Haven and we had the idea to have a boat show in our lobby. Imagine the customers' surprise when they came in to deposit their paycheck and were greeted by sleek, white power-boats. Our collaboration allowed us to throw ideas out to each other. On your own, picturing boats in a bank lobby might seem like a crazy idea, but when you are part of a team there is more permission to take a risk and offer ideas that might seem like they would never work. Our partnership was one filled with creativity and innovation.

MICHAEL JORDAN IS
CORRECT IS STATING
"TALENT WINS GAMES,
BUT TEAMWORK
AND INTELLIGENCE
WINS CHAMPIONSHIPS."

Before NCNB changed the way that banking was done in Florida, every bank had a president. Shortly after I arrived, a gentleman came into the bank and requested to see the manager. I came out of my office and introduced myself as the manager. He said, "No honey, I want to see the man." Well, I could have done two things. I could have quickly said "There is no president," or "There is no man." I'll admit a big part of me wanted to show this gentleman that the world was changing and now women were finally being given the opportunity to run things. But I realized that whatever my reaction, it wouldn't take place in a bubble. My staff was watching me to see how I would handle the situation.

I opted to add a little southern charm, and maybe I even exaggerated my accent a little. I said, "Sir, he's not in right now, but I would be glad to help you with your needs."

He smiled and said, "I know that accent. Are you from Georgia or the Carolinas?" I told him that I was from Georgia, and we had a great conversation. Instead of pushing a customer away because of my desire to make a personal or political statement, I was able to make him feel welcome and it ended with the client allowing me to assist him and in me becoming his banker. He never did know that he was actually doing business with the manager. All he knew was that "the man was not there."

The team was impressed by how quickly I turned a potentially negative situation into a positive one. I recognized that this wasn't the appropriate time or place to take a stand for women's roles in the business world, but I would have many opportunities to do so later. In this moment, what was important was connecting with a potential customer. It came down to the personal element that is the foundation of all great businesses.

The Winter Haven team was a great one. We truly functioned as a team and all worked together to grow. We were rewarded with the honor of being the number-one banking center in our region. I imagine that it was this success that led me to be tapped to be the District Manager in Sarasota about 14 months later which meant another move for my family. My husband's position was in Tampa, so whether I stayed in Lakeland/Winter Haven or moved to Sarasota he was able to be with the family. We did worry about how well the children would adapt, but they were sill young and adjusted just fine to their new elementary school.

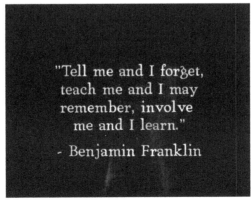

"Tell me and I forget,
teach me and I may
remember, involve
me and I learn."
- Benjamin Franklin

In my new position, I had half of the city of Sarasota and my counterpart, another woman in the work force, had the other half. Rather than trying to do each of our jobs in isolation, we sought out ways to use both of our individual strengths so that we could grow the market as a team. I really valued having another woman in upper management to work with. I've worked with many wonderful men, but their experiences in corporate America were very different than mine. Sometimes just knowing that someone is sharing in your experiences gives you the extra boost you need to make it through a challenging day.

My counterpart and I also learned by sharing our knowledge and experiences with one another. We didn't just tell one another what to do; in the field together we were able to model things for one another and we could immediately apply what we were learning.

Working in Sarasota is when I learned that my employer expected me to do all I could to make their business successful, but if I would do this, they too would support and invest in me. I've carried that knowledge with me throughout my career.

CHAPTER 3: MOVING UP

My phone was ringing and when I answered, I was surprised to hear the voice on the other end of the line and the news it announced. The president of the Florida division of NCNB was informing me to pack my suitcase for an adventure that could last up to three weeks. First I'd be going to Charlotte, North Carolina and from there I would find out my next destination.

There's something both frightening and exciting about being told you'll be traveling yet not knowing where you are headed off to. As I looked through my closet, wondering what type of weather I should be packing for, my mind raced with possibility. Soon some of my fears were abated.

In North Carolina, I found myself in a conference room with 120 officers from the company. At least I would have some company with me on this adventure. We were a group from all divisions of the corporation and soon became known as the "Top Guns." We were the team selected to go to Texas for the takeover of First Republic Bank Corporation. I felt honored to be selected as part of this group who were clearly the best at what they did. And I also felt that the hard work I did was being recognized. It meant a lot that the president of our company saw me as someone who was at the top of her field.

In the conference room, we learned our various destinations. This was before reality TV. We didn't exactly have a context for what was happening. Now there are shows where the music ticks like a clock as the participants wait anxiously to learn who is on their team, or what their task is, or where they'll be jetting off to. But for us this was uncommon and even extraordinary.

I discovered where I was going when I looked down at my airline ticket—Austin, Texas. I'd be going with several other young associates. We were given some instructions for what our roles would be. All of the "Top Guns" were part of a team selected to go to various towns and cities in Texas for the takeover of First Republic Bank Corporation. I was heading off to what became the first of the two biggest highlights in my banking career.

I was excited to be heading off to Austin with my team. I'd never been and couldn't wait to spend some time in such a lively place. The BBQ, the music, the thriving metropolis; I felt really fortunate to have been given such a great location.

Let me pause for a moment here to explain to those unfamiliar with the banking world a little bit about the industry. There are times when banks fail and the Federal Deposit Insurance Corporation (FDIC) steps in. No doubt you have seen the brass signs in banks proclaiming they are FDIC insured. That's to let you know your money is in a safe place. But the FDIC doesn't usually take over the bank; instead it's more common practice for them to give the bank to another bank that's bid on it. NCNB had bid on the failing bank and now it was our job to handle the acquisition.

Once we arrived in Austin, the process moved very quickly. We flew in on Thursday. On Friday evening NCNB was awarded the failing bank and by 7AM on Saturday morning we were meeting with the executives from the local bank. Twelve of the men we met with were in their fifties and sixties. I couldn't imagine how difficult it must have been for them. Chances are many of them had worked in this bank for their entire career and now they were facing a group of young people from another state telling them about the impending changes. There were also 12 young executives, or junior management, not too different from my team and me. We weren't even senior executives at the time, yet we were coming in to take over their banks. They must have felt anxious not knowing what changes would take place and what the implications would be. It was a very tense environment and my introduction to the first of many mergers that I would participate in during my career.

The first lesson I learned from this difficult acquisition was my admiration for those who chose to step up and shine in the face of this storm. This was a very tumultuous time for the bank. But despite the changes, many people rose to the occasion behaving professionally and with integrity. I saw that though we often can't choose our outward circumstances, we can choose the way we respond to them. To see people in the midst of shattering career changes or even loss of career maintain their composure, continuing to take on the work that needed to be done, showed me how sometimes all we have is our character and if we are fortunate, there have been people and experiences that have shaped this enabling us to meet challenges with dignity.

After our meetings with the bank presidents, we went to our respective offices to speak with the remaining staff. My goal was to assure those associates that they were still needed and that our company was a great one. Again, I drew on my leadership skills. In a way what I was required to do was like convincing a student that even though they may not like math, math will add value. But my work went beyond this. I wanted to let these employees know that NCNB was a great corporation to be a part of. I felt it my job to get them as excited about working for our company as I was.

All this time, knowing that Gary was home with our boys made it possible for me to do my job without having to be concerned about leaving my family. In the hotel room at night, I would often think of Gary and the kids, counting down the days until I could see them again. Even though I missed them terribly, I am so appreciative to have a supportive husband who has always understood how much my career means to me. And my sons quickly let me know that everything was fine without me, sharing how, "It was great with daddy. We had McDonald's and Taco Bell every night!"

While we were living in Sarasota, Gary received an opportunity for a significant promotion to move to Atlanta. I was torn because I loved my job, and the kids were doing so well in school. But Gary had made so many sacrifices for me and my career that I knew it was the right move for our family and was thankful to have an opportunity to support him in his goals in the way he had been so supportive of me.

I contacted our HR department in NCNB and was told that the only business that the bank had in Atlanta was their lockbox division, which just happened to need a manager. Though I was a banker by trade, I still had no idea what the lockbox was, but I loved my company and wanted to stay. Based on what you've seen in the movies, you might picture that I would be in charge of a room in the back of the bank with one of those two-ton doors that open with the turn of a massive wheel. I would walk couples and siblings to this room lined with boxes which they would open and discover within family valuables and secrets. But this is not at all what a lockbox division is.

Upon arriving at my new position in Atlanta, I set out to learn all I could about the lock box division. I learned that the lockbox team worked with large clients through our treasury to provide payment services. You know all of those checks or online payments that you send to your favorite department store, utility company, etc.? That is what the team was processing.

In everything I do, I want to understand the entire process. So I set out to work every shift and learn all the functions. If I had been placed in charge of a farm, I would have taken it upon myself to learn all there is about growing a crop. What type of soil is best for the vegetables? How much water do they need? What time of year is best for planting? Unless you get your hands dirty planting seeds, you can't know what it takes to grow a tomato. I worked every shift related to the lockbox division. This way I learned where I might make changes in the ways things were run. As a result, the team's production and accuracy levels went up, and the area became profitable. This did not happen without challenges, but we were able to persevere as a team and this is where I grew as a manager. I realized that life is a huge hill to climb, but the view is great.

During our Atlanta stay, I also became the president of my children's PTA. My memories of school government made me enthusiastic to take on a leadership position. I thought the job wouldn't be too different from the work that I was doing at NCNB, but I soon learned that managing people who work with you and managing volunteers requires a completely different skillset. What an amazing venture I had signed up for.

Managing the people that work for you every day, there's the understanding that your team normally has your same goals and your same agenda. Not so with volunteers. I soon realized that everyone in the PTA had different priorities. Some might feel that it's important to fundraise so that students can go on more field trips, while others see new soccer uniforms as a priority and still others want to buy more books for the school library. Parenting is a deeply personal task and so sometimes, people's own individual wants for their children would cloud their ability to see what might be best for the interest of the school and for all of the children. Some years later schools, like businesses, began composing mission statements and I think this can be really helpful. It gives the community a common vision to look to and can serve as a reminder that first and foremost, the reason we are involved in education is to provide challenges and opportunity for our children.

I've always believed in being precise and mindful of everyone's time, therefore at work or when running outside meetings, I've always worked to keep a time schedule. When I became more involved in my children's schools, I found that school meetings or functions could easily turn into a social gathering for the parents. Managing their time took a lot more effort on my part than I had anticipated. A simple fix I came up with was to tell parents, "We'll always keep on time. " I let them know that this was because I wanted to be mindful of their time as well as mine. I assigned someone to be a designated timekeeper to help keep the meetings on time. A trick I use in a business or club meeting, is to take off my watch and place it by my notebook. I still do that to this day. For one, it reminds me to keep moving forward with the meeting. But I've found that people really appreciate it when I take these steps to stay on schedule. I'm sure you've been at a meeting when people are shifting in their seats, tapping their pencils, checking the time on their watches or phones, anxious for the meeting to end. Keeping time actually allows people to pay more attention because they sense order. It says, "I'm mindful of your time, and therefore I'm going to keep this on track." Once they know that, they are free to pay attention.

I was still working different shifts at my new job to learn my team's job responsibilities and processes. At times, it was a midnight to 8 AM shift. I would come home exhausted from my changing work schedule and it was during this period of time, my youngest son, Clint, ended up contracting what was called osteomyelitis.

My son had injured his knee and not realized it, and it became infected. When we brought him to be treated for his infection, he had an allergic reaction to the medication, although we did not know it at the time. As my son's pain continued we were nervous that something was very wrong. There was the feeling that if the doctors couldn't quickly figure out what was happening to Clint, things might take a very dangerous turn. As a parent, you always want to be able to step in and rescue your child. Now Gary and I felt complete helplessness.

The doctors in Atlanta were finally able to realize what was happening. They told us that Clint had osteomyelitis, an infection and inflammation of the bone or bone marrow. He was prescribed additional medication to treat the reaction.

Clint was in the hospital from Thanksgiving through March. This brought back memories of our family's car accident and my own time in the hospital. Once again, we became all too familiar with the fluorescent-lit hallways, the constant background beep of heart monitor machines. This was not the life we wanted for our son. He went back to school for a brief time but then suffered a setback when he contracted an infection. He had to be pulled from school again to receive additional care. This was a huge disappointment for Clint. I think a lot of kids felt school was a drag. Maybe they even fantasize about not having to go to school. But all those months in the hospital bed, all Clint could think about was getting back to school and to live a normal life amongst his peers.

Fortunately we were back near our parents again. They provided support by looking in on Gary Jr. and just serving as a sounding board for me to get out my biggest fears. What if Clint never got better? What if things took a turn for the worse? I was an adult and yet it was still a comfort to have my mother nearby. Even with our parents help, either Gary or I would spend every night at the hospital with our son until we were able to bring him home.

When we brought Clint home, he still had a catheter that had been implanted in his chest and he could not go to school, so he was homeschooled. My heart broke for Clint. I wanted nothing more than for him to have a normal childhood. Eventually he healed, was no longer bedridden, and could go back to school. The episode was frightening but we came through the other side.

After these often-trying 18 months in Atlanta, I was asked to move to Greensboro, North Carolina to take over the retail bank in Greensboro. This was to be the first move that I made for NCNB where Gary and I were not together. This wasn't an easy decision. We'd learned from the ordeal that we had just been through with Clint, of the benefits of living so close to our family. Still, we weighed all sides and then made a conscious decision to have Gary remain at his position in Atlanta while I would take the position and move up to Greensboro with the boys. By this time I was moving up very quickly in my company and clearly, this would be a good career move. I don't for a second take for granted how fortunate I've been to have married a husband who recognizes how important it's been for me to grow in my career. I can't imagine what my life would have been like had I married a man who didn't support me in my dreams.

Off to Greensboro I went with the kids, and we settled into a home close to my office. By this time, the boys were in different schools – Clint was still in elementary, and Gary was in middle school. Living apart from Gary was a major adjustment. The children were just seeing their dad on the weekend, and during the week I was mom, dad, working executive, and taking part in the activities at both schools. I was truly trying to be all things to everyone.

I was starting to feel like life was crumbling in on me. I thought that maybe if I just tried harder, I would be able to manage career and home. This is when I first heard of the quote "Never get so busy making a living that you forget to make a life", and I realized although I enjoyed what I was doing, this was probably the most unhappy we'd been as a family. I think a lot of women in my generation were raised thinking we could have it all and do it all. We are now beginning to understand that this just isn't how life works. There are certain things that are sacrificed when we choose careers that are fulfilling but also call us away from our family. If we choose to stay home, we might sometimes wonder what life would be like if we had a career that we loved.

During our days in North Carolina, NCNB bought C & S Bank, and I was again asked to move. This time I moved back to Atlanta. Both the boys and I were thrilled to go back. They had many friends in Atlanta, to them it was home. For me, I was anxious to be back with Gary, to have someone to share the responsibility of parenting with. I could talk to him at the end of the day about work or the boys. Sure, there is the telephone, but it can't serve as a substitute for talking with someone and looking them in the eye, or observing the way they walk or talk that is unique to only them.

Though I had no question that taking the position in Atlanta was the right thing because it was what was best for our whole family, I loved the position I'd held in Greensboro and had doubts as to whether or not the position in Atlanta would be a good fit. So in a sense, I had to go out on a limb by moving back to Georgia. But I knew the fruit was on this limb.

Being a family is more important than the money you make to support them. Putting the needs of your children, your spouse, and the needs of yourself first is the key to being successful as a family.

Rita Lowman

CHAPTER 4: CHANGING GEARS

In 1993, Gary was transferred back to Florida. By now both of our boys were teenagers and they loved Atlanta. It was becoming harder to just pack up our home into boxes, pile into a car and relocate. Each time we were faced with moving there was a lot to weigh, but now the boys had many close friends in Atlanta and were thriving so we had the added consideration of reflecting on how this move might impact them.

When presented with the option to move, Gary and I have always looked at every angle. Ultimately, we want to make the decision that will be best for our whole family. After having lived apart once when the boys and I were in Greensboro and knowing what a stress that put on me, we knew we didn't want Gary to relocate to Florida without us. And it seemed really important for Gary's personal and professional growth to stay with the company. So many decisions had been made for my career, that I was anxious to be able to do what I could to support Gary in his career. And even though we knew the boys would be upset and angry when they learned of the move, there are also ways in which such a move can be a positive for children. Meeting new people and finding oneself in new situations is part of life. In a new school, the boys would have to make new friends and this, we felt, would be a good experience for them. We were also modeling for them sometimes one's career requires sacrifices. Of course we still wanted to do all we could to give the boys a happy upbringing. So we found a neighborhood with good schools, that was filled with kids and built a house there.

Meanwhile, I contacted NationsBank and they offered me a position to manage what was called "Project 93." This entailed bringing all of the banks we purchased into one bank—it was a corporate-wide plan. The project looked at cultures, policies, processes, staffing, and more. When one purchases a bank, or any company, I've found it is wise to see what that bank or company might already have in place that works well. There is a lot that can be learned from acquiring different companies. In Project 93, we didn't want to just come in and blindly place our preexisting policies onto these new banks. Rather, we wanted to look at the best that these other banks had to offer and to blend this together to make NationsBank. This really appealed to me, because I have always enjoyed looking for ways to build on the success of individuals and this was doing the same thing but at a company level. I was tapped to manage this project, and as a team we were able to complete a two year project in nine months.

During my time on this project, I also had the opportunity to really get to know a colleague who would later became my mentor and friend. She was the highest ranking woman at NationsBank, Alex Sink, and an amazing person to work for. In the early 90s, and still today, there are too few women in the business world and even fewer in high-ranking leadership roles. When I was fortunate enough to work with one I was grateful for the opportunity. I've had outstanding male mentors too and they've helped me but in different ways. Alex could understand some of the challenges that women face, but she didn't harp on these, she was very positive and encouraging. She stressed the importance of following my own inner voice. Like me, she had set out on a path that few before us had traveled. All sorts of messages are sent to women who work to excel in business—some of them encouraging and others full of doubt and skepticism. Can a woman really do this job? Won't being a mother get in the way? With all of these opinions, it is easy to question yourself. Alex taught me that the most important voice to follow was my own.

Well by being so efficient, I had worked myself out of a job in nine months. I was fortunate enough to then become the State Administration Executive for NationsBank for the state of Florida. In that position, I began managing operations, transition teams, and sales teams as a bank. We were buying other banks in the Florida market and merged five banks into NationsBank in three years. This was a huge undertaking. However, it was gratifying. The initial experience that I had with mergers in Austin when I worked for NCNB served as a great foundation for the work I was doing now. What I liked about this kind of work was that it gave me the opportunity to grow my project management skills. One avenue of the work required me to continue to find effective and positive ways to interact with people—both on my team and also the employees of the banks that we were acquiring. But there was a more technical element too, the focus and attention to detail required to consolidate several banks into one. Each aspect appealed to me and presented their own unique challenges.

I remember walking in to a very tiny bank. There were only a couple of tellers and it felt like I was walking back into time into one of those banks you see in a Western or some old movie, where ranchers or farmers come to get an advance when the crops are bad. We were acquiring this bank because we needed it in order to merge small banks along the East Coast into one corporation. The way state requirements work, NationsBank had to have operations close to each state line. That way we could merge Florida with Georgia, and then we could merge Georgia with South Carolina, and South Carolina with North Carolina. If I didn't have this position, I probably never would have known everything that it entails to grow a bank. I loved learning more about the regulations because it helped me see more of a behind the scenes look at the banking industry. I could have read all about these different state requirements and regulations, but having firsthand knowledge of them made it more tangible. Later, I could draw on this experience in some of my other positions. Really in everything I've done, I've learned initiatives that I used as I continued to grow in the industry.

Anyway, I walked into this bank and I was sort of shocked to see that they still had ledger cards. This would be like walking into a library and seeing an old card catalogue instead of a row of computers. For those that may not know, a ledger card is a card on which you physically write out, "Rita Lowman has borrowed $500." Then, each week when Rita would come in to make a payment on the loan, the banker would use the ledger card to record the $10 payment that she made or if she borrowed more money, it would be added on the ledger. This had been standard practice, but in the '90s when I was working on these mergers technology had started changing the way everything, including banking, was done quite a bit.

It would have been easy to have walked in the bank and judge their system as old fashioned and inefficient. I think a lot of people who might have spent more time in cities and in corporate America might have been tempted to see the way this bank operated as simplistic and a little backwards. But of course, I had come from a rural upbringing and I understood that the people working in this bank most likely felt that the way they were doing things had always worked fine, so why change? Rather than coming in and making changes from the start, I took the time to ask them about the way they recorded transactions. I said, "Well share with me what these cards are over here." They were very proud of the fact that when Joe Smith needed to buy a new calf, or somebody needed to get a part for their tractor, they'd come in and borrow $500. They, like me, understood that banking is about community. They thought that recording $10 weekly payments on a ledger card was a perfectly effective way to keep track of the money Joe Smith owed them. Part of our job was to share with the team there that there was a better, faster way of processing cash advances and helping them to feel comfortable with these changes as we updated their system.

During this time we also incorporated what is now known as the staffing model. The model was a predictor of when staffing was needed, allowing for no more than a five minute teller wait or a ten minute platform wait. Again, it is important to always remember that what we are doing is about giving the customers better service. That's an integral part of any successful business, banking or otherwise. At a glance, I'm sure it appears that mergers are mostly about the banks and executives at the banks, but in order for a bank to have success, first and foremost they must consider their clients and their employees.

To be the Bank of Choice, we must be the Employer of Choice.

- One of my personal quotes I began sharing in the early 90's -
Rita Lowman

One of the hardest elements of my job came when we converted teams. I often had the task of figuring out the staffing concerns. Whenever we worked on a transition, I would have to determine what people were needed and where. This meant I also had the difficult task of determining which people to keep and which people to let go. Not only was I the one making this difficult decision, quite often, I was the person that was going in and sharing with the president of the bank that we had taken over that he or she was not being retained through the transition.

My managers felt that often I was the best choice to deliver the news due to my southern upbringing. We southerners are known for being polite and it was felt that we could be understanding. I tried to put myself in the president's shoes. The task was made a little easier because I knew that more than likely they sold their bank for a good amount. I understood that they might still have strong connections to the bank. After all, many of us spend more time at our place of employment than we do at home. And so much of our identity can be tied to our career. Whether it is our upbringing or something biological or a combination of both, I think women are often able to be compassionate to those who are going through a difficult time. It was never enjoyable to be informing someone that they were losing their position yet I saw that I could do this in a way that was sympathetic.

She took the leap and built her wings on the way down

During this time I found another quote that I really like: "Time's like a river. You cannot touch the same water twice because the flow that has passed will never pass again. So enjoy every moment in life."

Despite having to be the bearer of bad news at times, I enjoyed every acquisition we made. I was recognizing something about myself that I had always really known. In work, I am most satisfied when I am presented with new opportunities and problems to solve.

One of my favorite acquisitions was when we bought Intercontinental Bank in Miami in 1996. I had the pleasure of meeting the gentleman that ran that bank, and his name was Bill Allen, who came over and became our Vice Chairman at NationsBank. He was charismatic, but more importantly, he was a teacher. He took the time to share with me how to do things differently that would make me better at my job. In a way, this was a type of reversal from many of the interactions I was having with people in the workplace. I was used to being the one pointing out where improvements could be made. While this is one of the aspects of the work I do that I love so much, I hadn't realized how much I craved being around someone who could be an instructor for me. There is a very special symbiosis that occurs when you are able to both learn and teach at the same time, and working with Bill during these years was this type of experience. I would soak up his knowledge and observe his keen personal skills and then over the years I tried to emulate many of his traits. I believe it's important to learn from every person that touches your life. From some people, you learn the good things and from others you learn the things that you don't want to be a part of your life. From Bill, I learned many good things that I was able to use throughout my career.

IN LEARNING YOU WILL TEACH, AND IN TEACHING YOU WILL LEARN.

One of the main things Bill helped reinforce is that associates are more than just employees. They have families, they have issues, and they have unique talents and abilities—they all have something to give. Once I had an associate, someone that I cared about, who needed to purchase medicine for their child. Rather than coming and asking me for help, they took the money out of their teller drawer without saying anything. Unfortunately, the auditors came in that next business day to audit all of the tellers, and there was nothing I could do. Giving employees a means to be able to help them in their time of need was always a goal of mine. I never wanted to see anyone jeopardize themselves or their employment just to provide for their family. The incident of the employee who took money from the bank helped make it a goal of mine to set up an employee fund to be able to help in cases of emergency just like this one. At a very early age in my management career I learned the importance of always talking to our associates and of letting them know that if they ever have a personal issue to please tell their manager so we can help them to find a solution. I take an employer's responsibility to look after associates very seriously.

Again, it strikes me that banking and finance, like any business is truly about the people. In order for me to be an effective manager and in any leadership position, we need to know our associates. It's important not just to show them you care about their families and personal life, you need to also know why they are a part of your organization. Several managers had modeled this for me.

After NationsBank bought Intercontinental there were two associates who I knew I wanted on my team. One of them was a young gentleman in his early 20s, who was their security officer. I just saw some quality in him that I sensed would make him a great member of our team. I told him "I don't know what you're going to be doing, but trust me and come onto my team." He accepted my offer and we have worked together 20 years. Having interacted and worked with many people, I had an intuitive sense that he was a great fit for our bank. He took a leap coming to work with me, someone who he knew nothing about, but perhaps he too sensed something in me that he could trust. I've found that the projects I've worked on and businesses I work for are most successful when we focus on and look for the best in associates and find ways to give them opportunities to succeed no matter what their position.

—

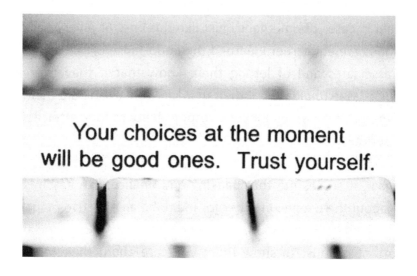

Your choices at the moment
will be good ones. Trust yourself.

In 1997-99 Alex Sink gave me a career opportunity that really stands out. I was able to be part of the Barnett Transition which was the largest transition that had ever been done at any bank at that time. We ended up closing 227 banking centers in one day and that had never been done in the history of banking. Of course, leading up to this, I was nervous as to whether or not we would be able to pull it off. We recognized what was at stake and that things could easily topple in the wrong direction if we made a mistake. One thing that was essential was to keep the retail staff engaged and working efficiently while these 227 centers were being closed. Of course when the day came to make the transfer, I couldn't be in each center at once. It can be nerve wracking in those moments when you have to trust that the work you have done is enough.

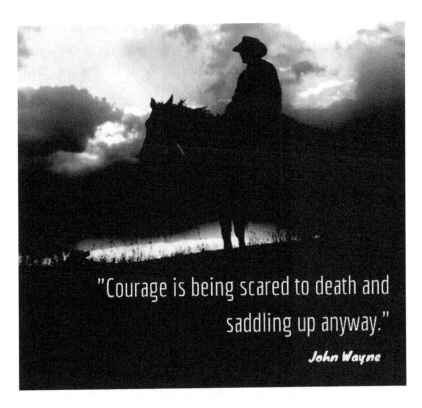

"Courage is being scared to death and saddling up anyway."

John Wayne

The fact that Alex gave me a major role in the transition meant a great deal. It showed she believed I was capable of such an important task. Once more we were tasked with navigating uncharted territory and someone who I respected was letting me know that she had confidence in my ability. This gave me the courage needed to step into that unfamiliar landscape.

When I received the Crystal Grenade from Hugh McColl—the highest award that he gave out each year—I knew that my work in the Barnett Transition had been essential. This is one of my proudest moments because it marked my ability to oversee major mergers and ensure that the transition happened smoothly and seamlessly.

Later after receiving that prestigious award, I decided to go back out into the retail side of banking and manage banks on the West Coast of Florida. During that time period, I was reminded of another favorite quote of mine that reflected my life at that point. "Little girls with big dreams become women with vision." It was my vision to continue to grow the retail bank on the West Coast of Florida. We currently had 100 banking centers and $5.8 billion in assets that was under my management. Soon after, our company became Bank of America, which is one of the largest and most well-known backs in the United States today.

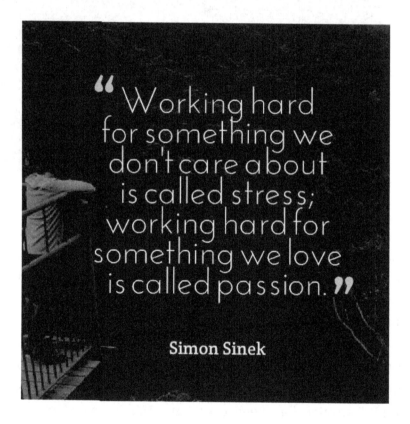

"Working hard for something we don't care about is called stress; working hard for something we love is called passion."

Simon Sinek

I've always loved my position in banking, working in big conference rooms with floor-to-ceiling windows and imposing oval wooden tables, that look like they would have no trouble filling up the space of a medieval castle. But there is a part of me that has also always been a farm girl at heart. I never abandoned my hometown roots. Since it appeared we would finally be settling down and not making any more major moves, Gary and I developed our cattle farm in Waverly Hall, Georgia, which is north of Columbus. We have 200 acres and still keep about 80 head of cattle on it. It's open country and big sky, a beautiful place where my whole family can be together and unwind. We love going to the farm to be reminded of the simple pleasures life offers, to enjoy each other and our time off.

On 4th of July weekend in 2000, I was helping Gary load the cattle onto the trailer to take to sell. My responsibility was simple -- closing the chute. I had a system and typically stood on the inside and closed the chute as the cows came through; it had never been a problem. As the last cow, weighing in at about 500 pounds, had gone through our dog Kilo spooked him. The cow turned and ran right back into me. I was trapped. There was no place for me to go and I knew I had no choice but to let him hit me. I braced myself for the pain as he tossed me in the air like a ragdoll. The earth raced up at me and I landed in a cow patty, but more importantly I landed on my right leg. This was the same leg that had been injured 17 years earlier in the car wreck. I knew it wasn't good when it swelled up immediately.

I yelled to Gary that the cow had hit me and knocked me down. He yelled back to "Get up and shake it off" I told him "There's no getting up and shaking it off." He finished loading the cows, and then came down to see what was wrong. He took in the sight of the cow poop and the swelling in my leg. I could tell he was trying to figure out the best way to get me to the house without messing up his car. A part of me was thinking, "just hurry up; can't you tell I'm in pain?" It added a whole other level of frustration. Gary ended up laying lots of towels down before getting me in the car. My leg was throbbing but we quickly cleaned up and headed to Hughston hospital, where the same doctors had taken care of me all those years ago. Once again I was brought into surgery, but this time I didn't have the added pressure of wondering how my kids and husband were. Fortunately, the surgery was a success –the doctors were able to repair my knee.

When you feel like quitting
think about why you started.

I returned to work a few days later. However, in a few short weeks while I was still on crutches, I, along with several other women, were asked to find opportunities outside of the bank. The bank I loved and gave so many years of my life no longer needed me. This was one of the many cuts , that associates would find themselves faced over the next few years. Still it was a shock. I had always loved my career and devoted my life to being a valuable and dedicated associate. I knew now how those people who had sat across the table from me felt when we had to tell them we were letting them go. This time I was not the bearer of the bad news, I was the recipient. There's really nothing that can prepare you for this chapter in your life. Even though I could tell myself that it wasn't personal, it was a financial decision, there is a sting that doesn't hurt less just because you know logically that your own performance is not related to your job loss. I had received a nice severance package but this can't serve as a cure for the reality that was sent my way. I had grown to love Bank of America, formerly NationsBank.

After the layoff I thought, I guess my banking career ends at Bank of America. I had given so many years of my life to banking, so many hours away from my family. Maybe this was a sign that I should take some time off. But I found I wasn't ready to give it up. From those initial days doing bank openings in Georgia, I'd always loved the business.

I immediately packed up, went back to the farm, and started sending out letters. Two weeks from the day that I left Bank of America, I received a call from Bill Klich, who was the CEO of Republic Bank. His call ended up changing my life forever. Bill gave me the opportunity to be the Executive Vice President over the majority of the bank. Bill was a true gentleman and another person who turned out to be a wonderful mentor. Like the best ones I'd had throughout school and my career, he saw something in me that he believed in.

I drew on a lot of the skills I'd acquired from my early years of banking. I oversaw the operations, the banking centers themselves, and marketing. It was an excellent opportunity to grow with a community bank. We had 74 banking centers statewide. Getting re-involved in the nuts and bolts of banking made me a better banker and a stronger leader.

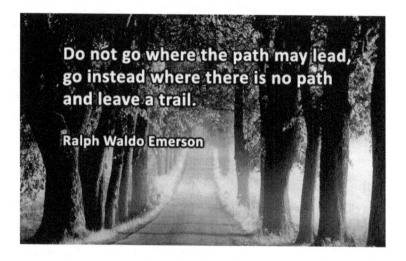

Do not go where the path may lead, go instead where there is no path and leave a trail.

Ralph Waldo Emerson

During that my time with Republic Bank, one of our goals was to make the bank healthy again. We knew that the primary shareholder wanted to sell the bank and we were able to get it ready to sell in only three and a half years. At that time, we sold the bank to BB&T and I chose not to stay on with the bank. I felt I had done what I challenged myself to do. Again, I knew enough about myself to know that I feel the most content when I have a completely new challenge to take on. In a way, though I didn't opt for a career in acting, I've still been able to perform a variety of roles. The play has never been dull or routine. It's a new show every night.

I first opted to help turn another bank into a sale opportunity in South Florida and this is what opened the door for me to take part in an entirely new role. I had the opportunity to actually start a bank, and that was another wonderful career changer for me. I was hired as the Chief Administration Officer for a de novo bank. We opened in 2006, and grew that bank from $100 million to about a $900 million in a 5+ year period. This was not something I ever would have imagined was where life would take me when the local newspaper interviewed me all those years ago and asked me about my career plans.

I WANT TO

inspire

PEOPLE.

• • •

I WANT SOMEONE TO
LOOK AT ME AND SAY

BECAUSE
OF

you

I DIDN'T GIVE UP.

I learned from starting a bank that people don't want to join a bank they don't know. It's a gamble for them to leave a job in a company that is well established. So to hire quality people was really a challenge. This was a new obstacle for me. I'd never had any difficulty finding qualified and competent people to work with me. Fortunately, over the years. I'd worked with some people who I knew believed in the work we did and therefore might be up for leaving their current positions to work with me. It is not like when you are working with people that you are saying if I should ever be a part of a start up bank these are the people I would take with me. But sometimes we find that people or situations from our past benefit us in ways we never could foresee. I thought of three or four people who had worked with me in the past who I wanted to reach out to. When asked if they would come work with me they all were willing to take that leap of faith with me. And so they did

Along with those initial people, we added several more. It was those first 10 people that really were the core of the team. Due to bank regulations, I had to personally hire the first 50 associates. The four executives hired were also responsible for picking out the computer systems, implementing them, and developing the product. This was the first time we had had the privilege for building something from the ground up. It gave me the opportunity to be a true entrepreneur.

During this period, the president of the Bank, and myself literally sat in a room, where we wrote policies and procedures for two or three months until we were able to get our charter and get the bank opened. We had to build the culture and vision for our bank so we wrote our mission statement and core values. It was a completely new experience. We didn't have anyone to turn to and say "Hey, will you help me here?" or "Can I get your take on this?" We always joked that if you wanted to see our team, you looked in the mirror and that's the team.

Talent wins games, but teamwork and intelligence wins championships.

Michael Jordan

CHAPTER 5: LEARNING BALANCE

During this time, my dad was diagnosed with cancer, and while I was working at the Bank he passed away from the disease. Any of us who have had to watch helplessly while a loved one falls victim to cancer can't help but look for ways to find better treatment or to end the disease. I knew I was good at raising money and it seemed a natural fit for me to find ways in which I could use these skills to help the American Cancer Society. My farming roots came in handy again and I chaired two of the Cattle Baron's Balls, and served as chair of Making Strides Against Breast Cancer. We raised $2.6 million at those events. I don't think it matters what one is passionate about, but I do feel that we should capitalize on our passions and use them not only for our personal growth, but also to give back to your community.

My other passion began when I started at Republic Bank as a member of the Florida Bankers Association. The Florida Bankers Association is a great organization, but as I became more involved, I realized two things: first, bankers in leadership positions tended to be men and secondly, I love to empower emerging leaders.

When I first joined the Florida Bankers Board, there were thirty-six members and only one female member. I would have been the second female, but the other female member was leaving which left just me. Since I was appointed to the board, we've nominated several other women, and we now have four women on the board. What is even more exciting for me is in 2017, I will be taking over as chair of the Florida Bankers Association, only the third woman in 130 years to hold this position. When I was young, there really weren't any women in the banking industry in positions of power. Young girls didn't really think of banking as a career except maybe to become a bank teller or a loan officer. By appointing women to the board we believe we can help to open up new doors for the next generation of women. Things seem within the realm of possibility when we see others doing them.

I'm equally excited about the opportunity that serving as the chair will give me the opportunity to bring more people into the Florida Bankers Association, and empower emerging leaders. In banking there is a large disparity in age range from tellers to executives. What is going to happen to banking when someone like myself retires? There is actually a great need to develop leadership traits in people in the banking industry. We've been able to bring emerging leaders in, through the Florida School of Banking where we train them to be future leaders.

We take these emerging leaders to DC and expose them to situations where they can experience what it is like to lead a bank or other organization. It's like the banking world's version of a medical residency or student teaching. We want to give them as authentic of an experience as we can so that they will feel prepared. Working to empower young people is another way that we can continue to give back. It helps them individually, but more importantly it helps the whole society when we invest in the next generation effective leadership skills.

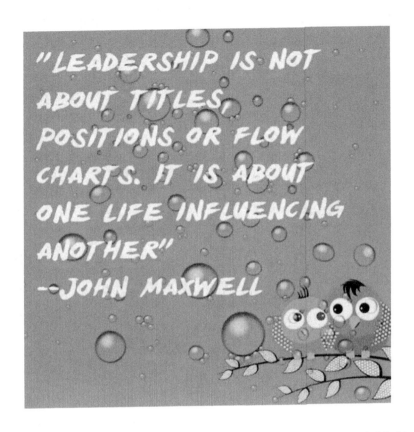

"LEADERSHIP IS NOT ABOUT TITLES, POSITIONS, OR FLOW CHARTS. IT IS ABOUT ONE LIFE INFLUENCING ANOTHER"
--JOHN MAXWELL

As my contract was ending with the de nova Bank, I started thinking about what I wanted to do next with my career. I had several banks that were interested in me. But only one bank really resonated with me—Community Bank of Manatee County. It had just been bought by a Wall Street entrepreneur, and the primary shareholder was from Brazil. It was being purchased from an excellent banker who was very well-known in the banking industry, and who was staying on as chairman of the bank. I was intrigued after I heard their story and met with the two primary shareholders. I realized I wanted to be a part of their growth. For me, it's more than just the success of a financial institution that draws me to want to be involved in it. Actually, sometimes it's been smaller banks that are in a position of transition and growth that appeal to me. What I look for in either case is that the people who are part of the bank are the type of people who I can see myself doing business with.

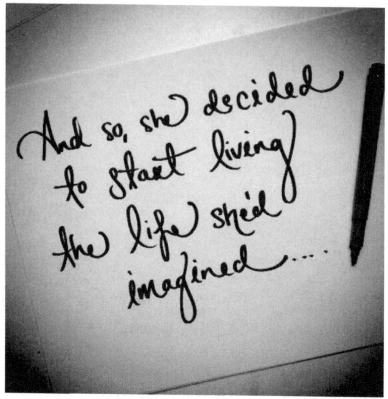

When I came on board, we were very small, a $250 million bank with only six or seven locations. In just under five years, we grew to a $1.6 billion bank with 32 locations. It's been a thrill to grow a corporation. It's really not unlike mentoring a person. In each case, you are taking something that already exists and finding ways to better capitalize on existing strengths. Just as I love being able to guide individuals I love the experience of working at an entrepreneurial bank. We are entrepreneurs and our mission is to provide opportunity for fellow entrepreneurs. So, we changed our name from Community Bank of Manatee County to "C1", which means "Clients First, Community First."

My work with the Florida Bankers Association made me aware of the necessity to train emerging leaders. At C1 we also introduced a management associate program to bring students who have just recently graduated, either with their undergraduate or MBA degree, into a program that was facilitated by the bank and University of South Florida St. Pete. When the associates finish a 26 week program, they had the opportunity to work for the bank or they could take their newfound skills that they've learned to another bank, or industry.

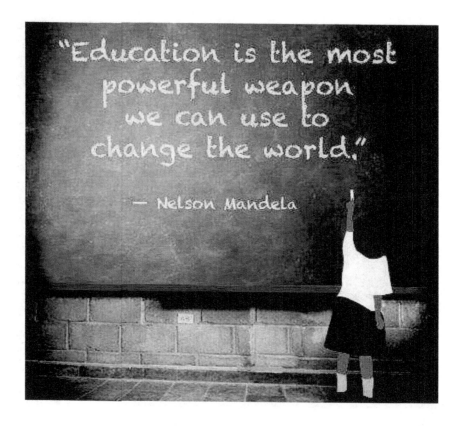

The management program was one of excitement and dedication for our associates. I have found joy in seeking ways to partner with different educational institutions to see how banking and higher education can support one another. Whether the associates we work with through the USFSP program decided to work for C1 or for someone else, it's been a pleasure to see them apply what they learn from the program in the real world.

One of the biggest things I realized while working at a true entrepreneurial bank is the importance of branding. Banks like NCNB, NationsBank, and Bank of America, have the advantage of already being well known. When we became C1 Bank, people did not know who we were. We had to be more innovative to get our name out there to draw people in.

I've always seen myself as a type of ambassador for the company where I work. We looked for creative ways to make sure people saw the team as part of the bank's brand, not only as the Rita Lowman brand. Whenever I am out in public, you will most often see me wearing bank colors. Plus, always try to represent your company at three to four functions a week. It is a great branding opportunity that is cost effective.

If you take a tour of Wrigley Field, you will notice that the cup holders behind each seat are emblazoned with the Bank of America logo. Obviously not all businesses have the kind of money to spend on high visibility marketing strategies such as this, but if you think outside of the box there are things you can do. And the principle is always the same—get yourself seen. We found ways to invest in the community with large and small events. We were one of the major sponsors for the breast cancer walk, *Making Strides*, and three of my banks have been the 'Bank of the Buccaneers', and we sponsor other smaller events too. It is all about being out in the community and people knowing who you are and what you are about.

It was while working at C1 that I experienced another highlight of my career, the first being in Texas with NCNB. This was when C1 Bank went public on the New York Stock Exchange. If you think of making it big in the United States, of starting small and growing your business, there's one iconic image that sums it all up. Ringing the bell at the New York Stock Exchange. It's been in countless movies and TV shows. It's truly come to symbolize making it big. When C1 went public we were in New York and wrung the bell! It was one of the two highlights in my career because of all that it represents for me and my aspirations. From a 4-H girl, I was now in the pinnacle of high finance.

I was able to have some very unique experiences with C1 bank. Four year ago we opened a bank in Miami with a completely different concept. Our CEO wanted the bank to serve as a showcase for us. He was very focused on the aesthetics- he wanted it to fit with our brand. However, when I looked over the plans I said, "You know, I still have to run a bank here." I saw that the concept was contemporary and really fit with the lifestyle and architecture in Miami, but there was no way it could function as a bank; there wasn't even a place for a vault. Here's yet one more example of how essential collaboration is. I was able to be the voice of reason while the CEO had the vision for a totally unique physical space for a bank. We changed the design to function as a bank during the day and a place for entertainment in the evening. The bank is a hybrid between a venue and a place to do business. The candy apple green that marked our brand emits a vibrant energy. We also hired people who were lively and intelligent, who had creative ideas. In this way we continue to generate excitement and enthusiasm for our bank and to bring in new customers. Once again, it comes down to being able to take a risk. I think back to the partnership with my old assistant manager and our idea to have a boat show in the bank. C1 Banks were unique and innovative and it kept me thrilled to be part of a company that pushes the boundaries of what we think of when we picture a bank.

We spent a lot of time trying to branding the image of C1 and make it a successful bank. You might see a space and feel it is cool and want to be a part of it. The trick comes in keeping you from thinking about all of the hard work that went into creating the store or the brand or the bank. When you eat perfectly made cake its fluffy and sweet and practically melts in your mouth. You don't taste the baking soda and the egg yolk. When you walked past a C1 Bank you didn't think of the construction or the meetings that went into coming up with the unique spaces. If we did our job right, you partake in an experience.

"Never get so busy making a living, that you forget to make a life."

Despite all the hard work that went into C1 and in all of my positions, I wouldn't change a thing about my career. I don't recommend that everyone make the same choices that I made. Each person's situation is different. People talk about how to balance your career and family. The truth is there is no secret formula. It was definitely a struggle to move apart from my husband and have our family separated for a short time. But it was important to me to be able to have a career and my family supported my goals.

There are going to be times when your career is pulling you in one direction and your family is pulling you in the other. Then you'll have to talk with the people who are important in your life and look inside and make the tough decision about which direction to choose. As I've shared earlier, I moved eight times in my children's first eight years of their school life. I started to see the toll this took on the rest of my family and my ability to enjoy the time I had with them. That's when I made a conscious decision on that ninth move—when my children were in high school – not to move again.

Life is so short.
Spend it with friends
who make you laugh
and feel loved.

There are some events in your child's life you may be willing to sacrifice but you are going to want to make sure that you experience their major events. One of the thing that's stuck with me over the years is something that Hugh McColl, who was the CEO of NCNB, shared with me. He said one of his biggest regrets was when his son made it to the Little League World Series, and he did not go to the game. He advised us to always attend those big events. He was right. There won't be a redo or a replay available if you miss the event. What I mean is, maybe you can live without making the game and try to catch a video of it on your spouse's phone later, but your child can't live without you being there. They see other parents who are able to show up and they understand that this a sign of love. They can't comprehend how important your meeting or deadline is, that you need to be there so that there is money for the Little League uniform. Hugh's words stuck with me and though I couldn't attend every game my sons were ever in, I made it a point to make the major events.

I have a word that's a favorite of mine and it's "CAUSE." The "C" is for "Commitment." You have to be committed to yourself and to what you truly want out of life to be able to be the best you can be. The "A" is for "Attitude". You have to have the proper attitude with everything that you are doing. If you don't enjoy and are not passionate about what you're doing, than you don't need to be doing it. The "U" is "Understanding." You need to understand the position and the job that you've been given. If you don't than you need to be able to ask "What is it that you're expecting out of me?" You also need to understand your commitments at home and to your family and make sure you have balance. The "S" is for "Self-image". You need to look in the mirror and like who's looking back at you. Learn to love who you are and embrace who that person is. Finally, the "E" is my very favorite, and that's "Enthusiasm". I've shared with my team for years that "You need to walk in and have that enthusiasm."

The "iasm" is "I am sold on myself". And I believe that if you're sold on yourself, then your company's going to be sold on you and that will help you to be the best that you possibly can be.

CHAPTER 6: OVERCOMING CHALLENGES

While I built my career and made sacrifices like working long hours, I always dreamt of one day having a place that I could enjoy. As much so as the boardrooms and the different houses where we lived as Gary and I pursued our careers, the farm has been a part of mine and my family's journey. We have a couple hundred acres of Georgia countryside, sprawling green fields dotted with 80 head of cattle and a nice lake. The boys have really enjoyed growing up there and I have too. It's my reprieve from the world. When I'm up there I can disconnect from the buzz of life, the many different directions I am pulled at work, and just focus on tending to the cattle and the land and being a farm girl.

One of the quotes that really resonates with me is "If you don't build your dream, someone will hire you to build theirs." Many of the things that I have done, I've been doing for other people but the farm was for my family and me.

I've also been building a dream as I strove to be a top banker and to find ways to make positive changes in our industry. One of the greatest pleasures I've had related to my career is to travel to DC and Tallahassee to share the different legislative bills that we'd like passed. I've met with Senators and congressional leaders to help inform them about what's important in the banking industry. Being involved in politics allows one to make an impact beyond one's self or one's business. It's also necessary to be informed of the current policies in order to make good decisions. When we started a new bank we had to be aware that there were different hiring procedures. Maybe I felt this made good business sense, or maybe I thought it was an unnecessary hoop to jump through. But beyond my own personal opinion, we have the ability to look at how this policy impacts the industry as a whole.

When I graduated from high school with nothing more than a high school diploma, as a woman, my options were limited. I stumbled into banking though it wasn't something I had dreamed of doing as a little girl when I was out there getting my hands dirty in 4-H camp. Because of the success I've had, I feel it a duty to help other women. There were few women in the banking industry when I began and this hasn't changed much in the past several decades. I benefited so much from people like Alex Sink who took it upon herself to act as a mentor. By working together, women have the ability to empower one another. I would suggest to women who are just beginning careers in business to find those organizations that have strong women in them or start your own organization that can bring women together. Recently, we had an event and I invited a young lady, whom I had just met, to the event. It was the first time she had ever been to an event like this. I received an email from her recently saying "Thank you so much, I would have not had that experience had you not taken me." Sometimes we might think a grand gesture is needed to have an impact. But it isn't just hiring a woman for the job that makes a difference. This woman's email reminded me that a simple act such as bringing a woman into a setting with entrepreneurs or philanthropists or CEOs might open up their world to new possibilities. Like the stone in a pond, your impact continues to ripple out as you are bringing others into your circle thereby connecting them to new circles.

While I find much inner fulfillment knowing that I give everything I do my all and in seeking ways to give others opportunities, it does feel wonderful to see hard work recognized. I've been blessed with the people I've worked with and honored with many awards in my career.

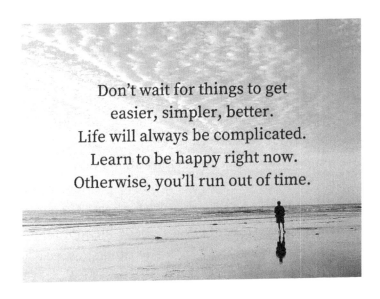

Don't wait for things to get
easier, simpler, better.
Life will always be complicated.
Learn to be happy right now.
Otherwise, you'll run out of time.

Don't wait for things to get easier, simpler or better. Life will always be complicated. Learn to be happy right now. Otherwise you'll run out of time. I feel that we are our own brand 24/7, and we need to make sure that we represent that brand in a positive way.

I had some opportunities when I was young that I know now were the result of good fortune and nothing special that I did. For instance, I was selected as a calendar girl for the city where I lived, so I got to be on the front page of the town paper which made me more visible and it wouldn't surprise me if this helped me as I looked for jobs or ran for leadership positions. But there were some downsides too; I received a lot of harassment over it. I learned that others don't always share in your joy. This hurt but it showed me not to put too much weight in how others respond to one's success. It also helped show me the type of person I didn't want to be. Rather it made me more determined to be nothing but supportive and positive to others; especially as I have continued on in my career.

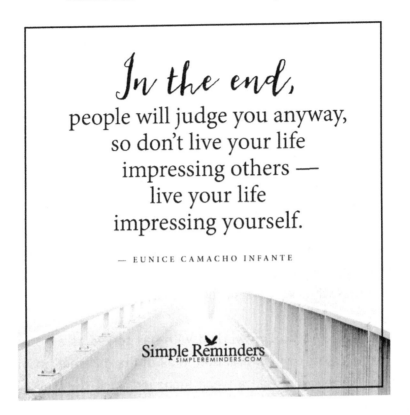

In the end,
people will judge you anyway,
so don't live your life
impressing others —
live your life
impressing yourself.

— EUNICE CAMACHO INFANTE

Simple Reminders
SIMPLEREMINDERS.COM

When I reflect back on the people who I have worked with and even some of the books I've read and the authors who took the time to write them, I realize how much I owe to other people. I hope that in some measure, I have had a similar positive impact on the lives of the people I interact with. We don't get where we are on our own. It's foolish to think this. Someone hires you, and in doing this they give you a chance. In that instance you receive an opportunity, which if you accept it with enthusiasm and dedicate yourself to, may end up steering the course of your life. A lot of the time we think about the partnerships we have with our spouses and our family and these may sustain us when work is challenging and overwhelming. But I have been blessed with also having people at work who I can connect with and I hope that in their connecting with, I have served as a source of strength, inspiration and understanding to them as so many of them have been for me.

I've seen how much good work can be done when we connect with people outside of our own workplace and in the larger community. I have the pleasure of sitting on several boards. In many ways these roles are similar to the one I took on when I was president of my son's PTA. As a local leader, we have the power to make a difference. However, it is essential to partner with others in order to capitalize on the strength available through making connections. I see how much more effective we can be by working with others in St. Petersburg, Tampa, and Clearwater. The more voices that speak up, the more powerful the message. We have a greater ability to help our communities when we form partnerships.

Not everyone who I've worked with has served as a positive role model. I guess its only natural that in all of the different positions we hold we will encountered a weak manager along the way. Some of them are overly critical of their team or fall into micromanagement. Others have difficulty delegating tasks and this makes the members of their team feel a project is being managed inefficiently. Believe it or not, people like for their own talents and skills to be used, so when one person tries to take on everything him or herself, it not only creates stress for that individual, it has a domino effect on everyone who they work with. Many times a poor manager will have such a negative effect on the team that competent, responsible, talented employees will leave. It's tempting to look at people who don't do their job well and criticize and judge them. Don't get me wrong, I've done it myself, but I think that we can go beyond our initial complaining and frustration and see these people as a type of signpost. Seeing a management style that I found to be detrimental, I would reflect on my own behavior and do a sort of check in to make sure that I wasn't falling into adopting any of those same traits.

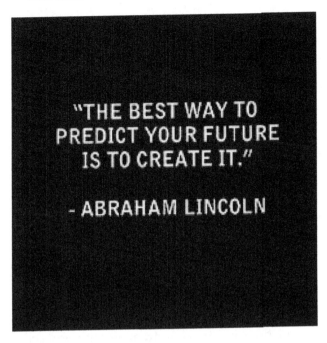

Not only associates, but clients are also affected by the people they interact with when conducting business. In this way, the people who work for you are really more important than the brand itself—clients don't necessarily bank with the brand, they bank with people. You've gone into a bank or even a grocery store and chances are, sometimes your experience is better than others. Maybe you are waiting in line and the teller doesn't acknowledge you because he is talking to his coworker. He motions you up without a smile and completes your transaction without any small talk. You might not want to come back to the bank. But had you been lucky enough to have the teller in the next window, you might have had an entirely different experience at the same bank. She greets you with a friendly smile and asks how you are doing. When you have a question about your savings account, she takes the time to answer clearly and thoroughly. Both associates represent the same brand, but one may lead to repeat clients while the other, sad to say may be the reason why people take their business elsewhere.

Life is about decisions. Choose wisely.

One of the biggest challenges I faced in my career was being the only woman in a boardroom. I had to overcome obstacles.

I remember sitting at the board table when the chairman leading the conversation would address the other gentleman by their names, and me as "Honey." I had to have the difficult and uncomfortable conversations with my male colleagues letting them know that "I have a name, and that name is 'Rita.' " I had to be firm and let them know that I expected to be called 'Rita' at a board meeting. These issues are going to come up from time to time and you have to know how to handle yourself correctly. Unlike the incident years before when the man came into the bank I let him believe that I was an associate because he couldn't conceive of a female manager. Now was the time for me to take a stand. I was there equal and I needed to speak up and insist that I be treated as such.

As women, we may fear that men see it as pushy when we stand up for ourselves. Or worse, we might worry that we are seen as unfeminine. I think it is natural for people to care how we are viewed by others, especially people we work with. But I wanted success in my career more than I wanted to be seen as a sweet, compliant woman. It's not that standing up for myself came easy, it's just that my determination to excel in my field was stronger than my desire for male approval.

The most recent group of area sales managers all happen to be men. That was not by design, it's just the way this particular group of area sales managers had worked out. I've had women and men as sales managers, but this group just worked out to be comprised of all men. Just because I feel passionately about giving women opportunities to move ahead in business, doesn't mean I hire only women. I always look for the people who are the best in the field. We always communicate as a team.

Life has many different chapters of story. One bad chapter doesn't mean it's the end of the book.

My early role models, excelled in their positions and were strong advocates of women. Finding our voices and our places in the business world means that we need to begin to feel comfortable being assertive and speaking candidly about our skills and abilities. Again, for

Girls compete with each other.
Women EMPOWER one another.

a woman we might feel that this is bragging. Honestly, there are times as I've been writing these thoughts about my experiences and a voice will say, "does this sound egotistical?" I question if a man has the same voice of doubt. There is absolutely nothing wrong with sharing and communicating the areas where you excel. Others modeled this for me. As it becomes more normal for women to speak openly about their skills and their accomplishments we may no longer think, "oh, its not appropriate for a woman to talk about herself like that." Instead it may become the norm for us to shine and feel proud as we talk about what we can do and what we bring to the table.

We need to take this even one step further. If you are willing to work hard and help grow that company , ask for that raise or that promotion. I moved up the ladder pretty quickly at NCNB, NationsBank, Bank of America but this didn't just happen. I gave my time and effort and proved the value I brought to these banks. In return, the company gave back to me. You should grow to expect this. You deserve to be compensated for the hard work that you do.

Because we were small bank, I held a number of positions at C1. Going back to my days when I became head of the lock box division, not knowing what the work entailed, I have continued to see the benefit of trying to work as many positions as possible (even if only for a short time) in order to really understand how a company or a particular division operates. I landed in a position at C1 that really suited me and allowed me to do what I love so much—interact more with the community. This wasn't possible when we were first growing our business but over time. We're able to bring in talented associates to handle some of the day-to-day activities.

Working for a smaller corporation is exciting in many ways. You have more of an opportunity for your voice and your vision to be heard. You can actually shape the company. But there are some things a smaller business can't provide. As long as I was at C1 Bank, no executive had an assistant. That meant that at 10 o' clock at night, I might be making my airline or hotel reservations. At larger banks, I always had an office and I always had an assistant. Sometimes I even had more than one. But the corporate culture has changed and continues to change. I've been able to stay in the center of banking for so long because I know the importance of being able to adapt. I have found that some people who came and joined us at C1 Bank from larger banks did not fit into the culture because they expected others to do for them what they needed to be doing themselves. Each company is different and not everyone will be a good fit at each place where they work. Not everyone you hire may work out well. I always tell people that if you do not fit into the culture or environment, it's okay to say "I need to move on." I admire people who are willing to speak up when they realize that the company or the job are not a good fit. It shows that they have self-awareness and know it is not worth it to waste their time or the company's time

What I have learned is the result of the many years I've spent in the banking industry. This didn't all come to me overnight. But as I have acquired more knowledge and arrived at some conclusions I share with others as it may help them to gain a deeper understating of the banking industry and the business world. Most of what I've learned is the result of me saying yes when opportunity was presented. Even though I may not always have been 100% qualified, I always remained open and willing to take on what my company asked of me.

Your own fears may prevent you from trying to do something that you are actually good at. At one point in our lives everything is new. We weren't born knowing how to walk or read or drive a car. Think of your job as just one more task that you have the ability to master. When we have a new job or elements of our job change, we may second guess ourselves. Some people say, "I'm not qualified" when asked about or given an opportunity. How do you know you're not qualified if you don't try? I always go back to the quote that "One day your life's going to flash in front of you. Make sure it's a movie worth seeing." In your movie are you sitting on the sidelines, or are you playing in the game? Even if you are not the star player, or your team is losing, you are out there on the field, playing, participating, part of the excitement.

It is so important that every step you've made has been one that you wanted to take. Now, every step I've made has not been calculated. But what has been calculated is the fact that I'm going to learn as much as I possibly can about the industry and I'm going to grow with the industry.

Don't wait for things to get better. Life will always be complicated. Learn to be happy right now, otherwise you'll run out of time.

Banking is so much a part of my life that I know even in retirement there is no way I can give it up. I also knew I wanted to be the chair of the Florida Bankers Association. This isn't a role that you can just apply for. It is given to people who have worked very hard to make a difference in the industry. Other bankers must believe in you and they do this by seeing your past accomplishments. I didn't take each of my jobs thinking that one day they would lead to this chair position. I took them because I love learning more about banking on every level, from legislation to starting a new bank, to best meeting the needs of associates and clients. It's never been enough for me to merely learn new things, I am driven to share what I learn with others. Not everything has come easily to me, but I have looked up to others for guidance and support. I say all this because these are the elements, which have allowed me to be given the honor of serving as chair of the Florida Bankers Association.

Never Look Back.

*If cinderella went back
to pick up her shoe,
she wouldn't have
become a princess.*

It is exciting to be engaging in a new chapter of my banking life. I am confident God has given me an opportunity to continue to learn, grow and lead as I move to my next adventure.

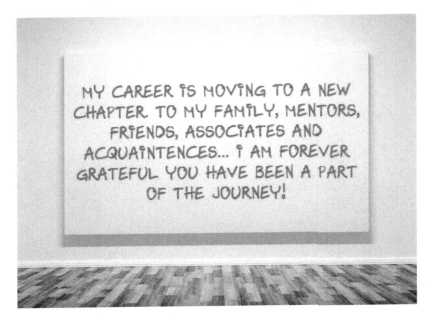

Rita Lowman

10 Leadership Thoughts I Have Used to Guide Life

1. Dream big and go for your dreams.
2. Ask for advice along the way.
3. Find the mentors/advisors who will guide you through your career.
4. Ask for the next step in your career.
5. Never stop learning.
6. Support those you love and they will support you.
7. It is okay to say no.
8. Love what you do.
9. Never look back.
10. Place your faith and family first ... always!

SUMMARY

In this book, I've shared with you the journey of my professional life. It was my goal to chronicle how I've grown as a leader, made a difference in the industry and been able to be a positive role model to young people. I found that just as it is a challenge to balance and juggle the personal with the professional, I wasn't able to write my whole life story in one book. So in my next book, I want to share more of my personal life, my family, and our triumphs in hopes of making a continued difference in others' lives. The sequel to this book and the next chapter in my life will share more about my children, how they've grown into adults and the issues that we deal with on those fronts. The second book will be coming out soon, and I hope that since you've enjoyed this book, you will pick up my next one as well.

ABOUT THE AUTHOR

Rita Lowman has been a banker for 40 years, blazing trails for the industry throughout her career. She currently sits on the Board of Directors Florida Bankers Association. She was elected to serve as the 2017 FBA Chair, Past Board of Government Relations, and Past Chair of the Education Foundation with Florida Bankers Association. Lowman was a past Board Member of the ACS Unit Operating Board for Tampa Bay and served as 2012-13 Chair for the Unit Board. She was also Chairman of 2012 and 2013 Cattle Baron's Ball. Rita is a member of the Board of Governors Centre Club and will serve as Chair in 2017-18. She was recently named to the American Bankers Association Community Council.

Elected to Board of Directors of the Outback Bowl for 2013/2014 and again for 2014/2015/2016. Rita was named Vice Chair of Board of Directors of the American Cancer Society's Florida Division.

Mrs. Lowman was also named 2015 Chair for Making Strides

Against Breast Cancer where the walk exceeded their goal with contributions hitting $750,000. Through Rita's leadership of the Cattle Baron's Ball and MSABC the American Cancer Society has had $2.6 million contributed to this worthwhile cause.

She served on the Fiserv National Premier Advisory Council and was named to the St. Petersburg Chamber Board of Governors in 2016 for a three year term. Rita served a three year term on the Board of Directors of the Florida School of Banking/University of Florida and was named as a Founding Member of the Women of the Bucs Life, an exclusive group of dynamic women to carry the Bucs and NFL message of recognizing the importance of women in the world of football.

She has had numerous articles on banking published and often speaks at state conferences on subjects from Successful Management to Women in the Boardroom. In June of 2014, she was recognized by the Florida Bankers Association with the coveted Chairman's Award. This prestigious award is given annually to a banker who gives back to the banking industry and promotes the goals and ideals set forth by the FBA. Rita was honored in 2016 as one of the Power 100 by the Tampa Bay Business Journal.

To contact Rita for speaking engagements or interviews, please visit her LinkedIn page: https://www.linkedin.com/in/rita-lowman-a541a910.

Rita Lowman

Made in the USA
Middletown, DE
24 May 2021